Generis

PUBLISHING

Mapping Out Unity: Theories and Trends in European Economic Integration

Monica Ariana Sim

Title: **Mapping Out Unity:**
Theories and Trends in European Economic Integration

ISBN: 979-8-89966-046-7

Author: Monica Ariana Sim

Cover image: www.ingimage.com

Publisher: Generis Publishing
Online orders: www.generis-publishing.com
Contact email: info@generis-publishing.com

FOREWORD

The European integration project, with its rich and multifaceted history, continues to capture the imagination of scholars, policymakers, and citizens alike. Over the decades, Europe has evolved from a war-torn continent to a model of economic cooperation and political unity, but not without intense debate and challenges. Theories of European economic integration provide crucial insights into how the process of integration has unfolded, as well as how it continues to evolve in the face of shifting geopolitical, economic, and societal dynamics.

This book, *Theories on European Economic Integration*, explores the underlying theories that have shaped the European Union (EU) and the broader European integration process. It provides an in-depth analysis of both historical and contemporary perspectives on integration, shedding light on key theoretical frameworks such as federalism, functionalism, and neofunctionalism. Each theory, while distinct, offers valuable tools for understanding the complexities of the EU and the ever-evolving relationships between its member states.

The work is structured to offer a comprehensive examination of these theories, starting with the foundational supranationalist models and moving toward more current trends such as multi-level governance and regional interdependence. It dives deep into the contributions of key figures such as David Mitrany, Ernst Haas, and Jean Monnet, all of whom played pivotal roles in shaping the course of European integration. Moreover, the book provides a critical examination of how these theories have influenced the European integration process and continue to inform debates on the EU's future.

In the context of an increasingly interconnected and interdependent world, understanding the dynamics of European integration proves important for scholars of European studies and anyone involved in international relations, economics, or policy-making. The EU, in its current form, represents a complex balance between the pursuit of deeper integration and the respect for national sovereignty. This tension is at the heart of ongoing debates on the EU's future, especially in the wake of crises such as the Brexit referendum and the ongoing challenges posed by geopolitical instability.

Theories on European economic integration are more relevant than ever, as Europe faces new challenges in terms of political unity, economic stability, and its role on the global stage. This book invites readers to engage with these theories critically and thoughtfully, providing a foundation for a deeper understanding of the forces at play in shaping the future of European integration.

As we continue to witness unprecedented change within the EU and across Europe, this work will undoubtedly serve as a valuable resource for those seeking to understand not only where the EU stands today but also where it might be heading tomorrow.

The author

Table of Contents

INTRODUCTION

The Finality Issue in the European Integration Process

The question of *finality*—or the ultimate purpose—of European integration has played an important role since the early days of the European project. Advocates of a united Europe envision a robust supranational entity characterised by shared sovereignty, leading to a unified European state capable of binding decisions across member countries. In contrast, adherents of intergovernmentalism argue for the preservation of national sovereignty, endorsing a cooperative framework where states collaborate on selected issues without ceding significant authority to centralised institutions.

The concept of varying integration models is well illustrated in the literature, particularly through the frameworks of multilevel governance and network governance, which examine how decisions transcend multiple layers of government in the EU. For instance, Goldsmith discusses the implications of variable geometry in European governance, noting that the evolution of the EU requires interaction across subnational and supranational dimensions, which are pivotal for structural integration in response to diverse political needs (Goldsmith, 2003). This model recognises the network of state relations that do not align uniformly with the traditional dichotomy of either federalism or intergovernmentalism. Instead, it champions a blended approach that incorporates elements from both, aligning with the fluid dynamics of European policy-making.

The early optimism of the integration process encountered significant setbacks with the onset of crises such as the *Luxembourg Compromise* of 1966, which restored national veto power in response to French concerns about supranational encroachments. The compromise made it clear that integration would not proceed in a linear, uninterrupted fashion. Instead, it became evident that progress would be contingent upon political will, shifting interests, and national sensitivities.

The next enlargements of the European Community, particularly the accession of more cautious or sceptical member states such as the United Kingdom and Denmark, compounded the challenge. These states were primarily interested in the economic benefits of a common market, rather than the political unification of Europe. As a result, the diversity of visions and motivations within the Union expanded significantly. This heterogeneity fostered a strategic ambiguity regarding the EU's ultimate objectives, resulting in a tacit consensus to avoid addressing the question of finality too explicitly.

For much of the 1970s and 1980s, the European project moved forward through pragmatic, incremental steps. Policymaking was often reduced to agreements around the lowest common denominator, and the broader political ambitions were largely shelved. Scholars and policymakers alike resorted to characterising the EU as a *sui generis* construct, unique and therefore exempt from traditional classifications of statehood or international organisation.

This vagueness became increasingly untenable beginning in the mid-1980s with the advent of the *Single European Act* (1986) and the *Maastricht Treaty* (1992), which laid the foundations for the European Union and introduced the Economic and Monetary Union. These developments reinvigorated the integration process but also heightened the need for a clearer vision. The dramatic political transformations of 1989–1990, particularly the fall of the Berlin Wall and the collapse of communist regimes in Central and Eastern Europe, further accelerated integration and necessitated decisive institutional adaptations.

The EU's enlargement into Central and Eastern Europe, culminating in the 2004 and 2007 accessions, posed new questions about the EU's identity, governance structure, and finality. In response, the *Constitutional Treaty* (2004) aimed to consolidate the EU's legal architecture, simplify decision-making, and symbolically affirm the Union's quasi-federal nature. However, the treaty's rejection in French and Dutch referenda in 2005 revealed deep public scepticism and signalled a failure to reconcile elite-driven integration with popular legitimacy.

The *Lisbon Treaty* (2007), signed in the wake of this setback, emerged as a more modest but pragmatic alternative. It retained many of the institutional reforms of the Constitutional Treaty (such as the creation of a permanent President of the European Council and the High Representative for Foreign Affairs and Security Policy) while avoiding overt federalist language. Importantly, it introduced the *principle of conferral*, reaffirming that the EU can only act within competences voluntarily granted by the member states—a nod to intergovernmentalist concerns.

In the present context, the ambiguity surrounding the EU's finality continues to influence debates on sovereignty, strategic autonomy, and the Union's role in global affairs. The COVID-19 pandemic, Russia's invasion of Ukraine, and growing geopolitical tensions have reignited calls for a stronger, more united Europe. Concepts such as *European strategic autonomy*, especially in defence, energy, and digital policy, have gained traction. These debates reflect an evolving understanding of sovereignty, not as a zero-sum principle, but as one that can be exercised more effectively through collective action.

Nonetheless, fundamental questions remain unresolved: Should the EU evolve into a full-fledged political federation with a common defence and foreign policy? Or should it remain a flexible, multi-speed union that respects national identities and divergent ambitions?

The tension between unity and diversity, between deepening and widening, and between supranationalism and intergovernmentalism continues to shape the trajectory of European integration. As the Union navigates current and future crises, the need to define, or at least to openly debate, its finality becomes increasingly urgent. Without a shared vision of its ultimate destination, the EU risks stagnation, fragmentation, or the erosion of public trust.

1. Supranationalist Theories

The discussion surrounding supranationalist theories in the context of European integration highlights two distinct forms of cooperation: intergovernmentalism and supranationalism, concepts central to understanding the complexities of European integration.

Intergovernmentalism emphasises the preservation of national sovereignty, allowing member states to collaborate while retaining their power. This is exemplified by institutions like the European Council, which relies heavily on consensus and respects the independence of national governments, often prioritising their preferences over collective decisions (Bickerton et al., 2014). In contrast, supranationalism involves the substantial transfer of sovereignty from member states to higher authorities, such as the European Union (EU) institutions, which implement binding decisions that transcend national interests (Genschel & Jachtenfuchs, 2015). The earliest instance of this paradigm in Europe is the European Coal and Steel Community (ECSC), which established a foundational framework for collaborative governance that curtailed national sovereignty in favor of shared interests in coal and steel production (Genschel & Jachtenfuchs, 2015).

This tension between intergovernmentalism and supranationalism in European integration is framed within the context of evolving legal and political structures. The establishment of the European Public Prosecutor's Office (EPPO) is a contemporary illustration of attempts to balance member state sovereignty with supranational judicial authority. While the EPPO is intended to enforce EU laws across member states, its operational effectiveness is complicated by limitations that reflect ongoing sovereignty concerns among nations, making it challenging to assert authority effectively (Schmeer, 2023; Ellinas & Suleiman, 2011). These dynamics indicate that the integration process is characterised by conflicts and negotiations over the distribution of power between national and supranational levels (Kohler-Koch & Friedrich, 2019).

1.1. Federalism

1.1.1. The Beginnings of European Federalism

Attempts at unification between states have been observed since ancient times. However, it was only in America, through the Philadelphia Convention of 1787, that the first federal constitution in history was created.

This was the result of a compromise between the movement that sought to unite the 13 declared independent colonies into one state and the movement that wanted to maintain the absolute sovereignty of the former colonies. Federal constitution-making represented a fortunate compromise because, as Alexander Hamilton acknowledged, it allowed the expansion of the representative government's competitiveness, achieving unity in diversity. With federalisation, the people were represented in Congress, while states could defend their own interests in the Senate. Thanks to the federal union, American citizens were able to experience brilliant economic development and, more importantly, avoid the contradictions and wars that continued to plague the great powers of Europe and countries in South America, which, once they gained independence, struggled to follow the path of political unity. Thus, following the American model, during the Resistance, opposition groups began to form in all European countries to rebuild a pacified Europe, free from racial hatred and borders. In the post-war period, European governments were unable to guarantee economic independence or the security of their citizens autonomously.

The idea of European federalism, which in the 19th century was considered a noble ideal, became a concrete political project. In the Ventotene Manifesto (1941), "the line of separation between progress and reaction" was drawn between those who aimed for the federalisation of Europe as a priority political objective and those who believed that the values of freedom, democracy, and social justice could be achieved within a national state. For this reason, the European Federalist Movement was founded in Milan on August 27-28, 1943, a movement quite radical in terms of its solution for Europe.

Federalists were convinced of the necessity to question the existing political arrangements in Europe. They prioritised making formal changes to the structure of political institutions and methods of action as a key element in ensuring social security and democracy. As a doctrine, federalism was always more concerned with formal aspects and finding an appropriate institutional framework to harmonize social diversity with the need for better governance than with the integration process itself.

For them, political change was the direct consequence of changes in public attitude, with elites playing an important role in this matter.

Ideologically, federalism is placed within the liberal–idealist tradition of international relations, starting with Kant's work, continuing with Woodrow Wilson, and reaching the present day through voices such as Richard Falk, Daniel Held, and Danielle Archibuggi. Some of the favoured themes of liberals, such as concern for diversity or the role of elites, are an integral part of federalist discourse. Although its historical origins lie in the Enlightenment, the federalist movement began to articulate only at the end of World War I. Several factors are considered important and decisive in this regard: the horrors that military technology can cause to people, the emergence of a key player on the international political stage – the United States of America, the impact of the Russian Revolution, the spread of fascism, and unprecedented economic and social changes. All these ideas and events led to a crisis of European values and created fertile ground for the rise of the European unification movement.

During the interwar period, federalism managed to gain support from a wide range of the European intellectual elite, with political figures such as Thomas Masaryk, Engelbert Dollfuss, Aristide Briand, Karl Renner, Gustav Streseman, Nicolae Titulescu, cultural personalities like Paul Claudel, Selma Lagerlof, Thomas Mann, Miguel de Unamuno, Ortega y Gasset, Salvadore de Madariaga, and scientific personalities such as Sigmund Freud and Albert Einstein.

After World War II, politicians such as Winston Churchill, Robert Schuman, Charles de Gaulle, and Konrad Adenauer reconsidered federalist ideas. Altiero Spinelli and Ernesto Rossi used federal ideas to mobilize resistance against Nazism. The Ventotene Manifesto, written by Spinelli and Rossi, became a common platform for action for resistance fighters and took inspiration from interwar European federalist ideas.

At the end of World War II, although federalism seemed to be well-placed both as a political movement and as an ideology, it was definitively removed from the sphere of public interest after the British political class rejected any structure that would threaten national sovereignty. The collapse occurred in 1956, when, following the failure of the Pleven Plan (1954), the federalist movement split. On one extreme was the radical European Federalist Movement (EFM) under the leadership of Spinelli, while on the other was the more pragmatic European Federalist Action (EFA). The emergence of a new experiment in regional cooperation in the form of the European Coal and Steel Community began to gain ground, even receiving support from the more pragmatic wing of federalists. The European Federalist Movement remained hostile to any concession in favour of achieving the ideal of a federal Europe through any means other than the classical, constitutional path.

Traditionally, federalists have advocated for the creation of a supranational entity in which power would be distributed across multiple levels of separate, yet coordinated, authority: the federal level, the governmental level, and (the regional level) and the local level. The political system thus structured would be based on a constitution that guarantees cultural and social diversity, as well as the autonomy and integrity of the constituent states, while ensuring unity and homogeneity across the whole. Thus, the idea of a constitutional arrangement came to occupy a central position in federalist discourse.

However, within federalists, there is no unity of opinion regarding how the federation should be achieved, the constitutional arrangement, and the division of power within the federation. Some argue for an abrupt shift to a constitutional arrangement based on a federal constitution, while others support a gradual move to a federal organization by creating popular movements around the elites in favor of federalism and only then moving on to the development of constitutional arrangements that would enable the new political system to function. Among the supporters of this view is Amatai Etzioni, who defines federalism as "a process whose end goal is the creation of a political community capable of controlling the means of using force, having a decision-making center with authority regarding the allocation of resources and rewards at the community level, and enjoying recognition of its political authority by a large majority" (Etzioni, 1965). The author examines the challenges of achieving a truly federal Europe, highlighting issues such as the lack of a unified political identity and the dominance of national interests over European integration. While the EU exhibits some federal characteristics, it remains primarily intergovernmental, with member states retaining significant sovereignty.

Criticism directed at federalists relates, first and foremost, to the inability to draw a clear line between advocacy and theory; secondly, to the fact that the final result of integration, from the federalist perspective, would be the creation at the European level of an institutional order similar to that existing at the state level. Thus, the problems that arise are determined by the increased distance between governors and the governed, by "the extension of inter-regional rivalries to a continental scale through the creation of a super-state that would practically reproduce, on a larger scale, the weaknesses of the political order existing based on nation-states" (Etzioni, 1965). Another criticism concerns the form this future federal Europe should take, which is not established by federalists. In recent years, three possible answers have been proposed:

- Transforming current states into components of a system similar to the United States of America, the German Länder, or the states that make up the Canadian federation;
- Differentiated integration or a Europe characterised by varied integration models, with the depth of integration varying from case to case;
- A Europe of regions characterised by two regional levels of governance: one sub-national and one European.

Its conceptual elasticity makes federalism a tool used in a series of political projects, with its influence being felt in the principles and procedures for achieving European integration, exemplified by the principle of subsidiarity enshrined in Article 3b of the Treaty on the European Union. Looking ahead and analysing the events of recent years, the number of member states, and the configuration of EU institutions, we can say that Europe is inclined toward federalism, whose importance, according to Michael O'Neill, who discusses the role of federalism in balancing diversity and political coherence within governance systems, lies in its capacity "to offer a balance between diversity and the degree of political coherence absolutely necessary to ensure stability, to create a correspondence between democratic representativeness and social plurality, on one hand, and political order and efficient yet equitable distribution of power within governance, on the other." (O'Neill, 1995) It is clear to us that the European Union already has several federal traits:

- Its constitution, formed by a series of treaties, creates the institutional framework;
- European citizenship;
- The guarantee and protection of the formal rights and freedoms of citizens, realised with the adoption of the Treaty of Nice;
- The European Court of Justice is empowered to guarantee and interpret EU legislative documents;
- The Council of Ministers has the capacity to adopt legal documents that take precedence over national legislation and are binding for all;
- The directly elected European Parliament has the necessary prerogatives to supervise the activities of the European Commission. The European Commission is the executive body of the EU, and its main competencies are control (ensuring the respect of the Treaty), initiative (it holds a monopoly on the initiative in matters of community competence), and representation

(internally, by presenting credentials to ambassadors from various countries to the President of the Commission, and externally through Delegations with embassy rank in candidate or third-party countries, as well as offices in EU member states);

- The institutions include a federal judicial system: a legislature in which Parliament, representing citizens, has growing legislative power, while the Council, which represents the states, is the most powerful legislative body and dominates internal and external security policy; the executive – the European Commission has considerable federal competences, although, in this regard too, the Council maintains control.

The success of the federal constitution can be attributed to its ability to foster economic development and political stability. The system helped minimise conflicts that commonly arose in other regions, where newly independent nations frequently grappled with achieving political unity (Powers, 2022). The U.S. avoided many of the wars and frictions that characterised the relationships between these nations, leading to a stronger and more cohesive state that prioritised collective governance. This has prompted scholars to reflect on how the U.S. experience in establishing federalism bears historical parallels with contemporary discussions on supranationalism in Europe, where the tension between national sovereignty and political integration remains a significant concern (Митин & Lebedev, 2024; Harbers et al., 2021).

Inspired by the American model, during World War II, resistance movements across Europe began to promote the idea of a pacified Europe, free of racial hatred and national borders. In the postwar context, European states were no longer capable of ensuring economic prosperity or guaranteeing their citizens' security in isolation. Thus, the concept of European federalism, once a lofty ideal of the 19th century, transformed into a concrete political project. In the 1941 *Ventotene Manifesto*, the line was drawn between progress and reaction: between those who prioritised European federalisation and those who believed that values such as freedom, democracy, and social justice could only be achieved within the framework of the nation-state. This foundational vision led to the establishment of the European Federalist Movement in Milan on August 27–28, 1943—a movement notable for its radical stance.

Federalists believed that the existing political order in Europe needed to be fundamentally restructured. They emphasised institutional reforms as key to safeguarding democracy and social security. More focused on institutional design than on the gradual integration process, federalist thinkers viewed political transformation as driven by shifts in public opinion, with elite actors playing a vital role.

The 1943 establishment of the European Federalist Movement in Milan represented a radical step towards political restructuring in Europe. Federalists argued that the existing political order required profound reforms to safeguard democracy and social welfare. Emphasising institutional designs rather than gradual integration processes, they believed that shifts in public opinion, spurred by elite actors, were crucial in driving this transformation (Kaplan, 2018). Their ideas resonated with influential figures at the time, such as Winston Churchill and Robert Schuman, and were rooted in the liberal-idealist tradition of political thought, tracing influences from Immanuel Kant to contemporary scholars like Richard Falk and David Held (Beyers & Bursens, 2013).

Ideologically, federalism is situated within the liberal–idealist tradition of international relations, tracing its roots to Immanuel Kant, continuing through Woodrow Wilson, and extending to contemporary scholars such as Richard Falk, Daniele Archibugi, and David Held. Central liberal concerns, such as managing diversity and the role of elites, are embedded in the federalist narrative. Though Enlightenment ideals laid the intellectual groundwork, European federalism truly began to gain momentum after World War I, influenced by disillusionment with war, the rise of the U.S. as a global power, the Russian Revolution, the spread of fascism, and rapid socioeconomic changes. These factors exposed a crisis in European values and provided fertile ground for federalist ideas.

Despite its early postwar prominence, federalism lost momentum after Britain rejected supranational structures that threatened national sovereignty. A major setback occurred in 1956, after the failure of the Pleven Plan (1954), when the federalist camp split into two: the radical European Federalist Movement (EFM) led by Spinelli, and the more pragmatic European Federalist Action (EFA). Meanwhile, pragmatic federalists began to support the emerging European Coal and Steel Community (ECSC), though the EFM remained opposed to any method other than a classical constitutional path.

Historically, federalists have advocated the creation of a supranational system in which power is distributed across multiple levels—federal, national, regional, and local. Such a political structure, grounded in a constitutional order, would protect cultural and social diversity while ensuring unity and cohesion. Nonetheless, federalists have not reached a consensus on how to achieve such a federation or how powers should be allocated within it. Some favour a rapid transition to a federal constitution, while others advocate a gradual path, led by elite-supported popular movements. Among the latter, Amitai Etzioni defines federalism as "a process culminating in the creation of a political community capable of controlling the use of force, allocating resources at the community level, and enjoying broad recognition of its political authority." (Etzioni, 1965)

Criticism of federalist theory is twofold. First, it is often unclear whether federalism serves as a normative advocacy platform or as a coherent theoretical framework. Second, critics argue that a European federal structure could merely replicate the limitations of the nation-state model on a larger scale, exacerbating the gap between governors and governed and extending inter-regional rivalries across the continent. There is also ambiguity regarding the final shape of a federal Europe. Three possible models have been proposed:

- A federation modeled after the U.S., Canada, or Germany;
- A differentiated Europe, where integration levels vary among member states;
- A Europe of regions with governance occurring at sub-national and European levels.

The EU exhibits features of a federal judicial and political system. The European Parliament (representing citizens) and the Council (representing states) jointly legislate, while the Commission serves as the executive. Amid debates over centralisation versus subsidiarity, the Maastricht Treaty enshrined the latter principle in Article 3b, which limits Community action to areas where national objectives cannot be effectively achieved alone but can be better attained through collective action.

1.1.2. Federalism, Cosmopolitanism, and Nationalism

During the same years that the American colonies were heading toward independence and union, philosopher Immanuel Kant concluded that war, and not law, was the only path states could take to achieve justice in the anarchic situation in which they lived. Therefore, true international law would not exist until states abandoned the idea of wild liberty in which they existed and accepted a common constitution, that is, a government with enough power to ensure universal peace and the independence of each member state. He argued that true international law could not exist until states relinquished their unfettered sovereignty and adopted a common constitution—a form of governance with sufficient authority to ensure both universal peace and the independence of its member states.

The cosmopolitan value of federalism, implicitly expressed through the American constitution and explicitly in Kant's thinking, is suffocated by the strong rise of nationalism. The cosmopolitan value of federalism—implicitly embodied in the American Constitution and explicitly articulated in Kant's philosophy—was soon overshadowed by the ascendance of nationalism. The rise of the nation-state often suppressed local autonomy and marginalized ethnic minorities. Relations among states came to be defined predominantly by power dynamics and national self-interest, with states demanding absolute loyalty from their citizens, even to the point of sacrificing their lives.

From the federalist perspective, the national dimension of the state is increasingly inadequate for addressing the pressing global challenges of contemporary society and for ensuring effective citizen participation in governance and the efficient organisation of political space. Federalists argue that the nation-state must cede certain competences—either upward, to a European or supranational level, or downward, to territorial units such as regions, municipalities, or communes.

Federalism agrees to organise the relationships between different territorial communities democratically, from the lowest level (regional) to the national or continental level. Through a union of different continental federations, the creation of a democratic world government becomes possible. Federalism envisions a democratic organisation of governance across various territorial levels, ranging from local to national and continental. The ultimate goal is the formation of a democratic world government, potentially arising through the union of continental federations. The division of power between the different levels of government must be respected:

- **The principle of territorial subsidiarity**, which dictates that issues should be addressed at the most immediate or local level capable of resolving them effectively, with higher levels intervening only when necessary;
- **The principle of territorial solidarity**, which asserts that citizens of wealthier regions have a responsibility to support the development efforts of less affluent communities, thereby fostering greater equity and cohesion across regions.

1.1.3. The State in Federalism

The birth of the federal state coincides with the founding of the American Federation in 1787. The text of the United States Constitution, approved at the Philadelphia Convention on September 17, 1787, is, in fact, the first example in history of a federal constitution.

The 1787 Constitution is, in reality, the result of a compromise between those who wanted to create a unitary state among the 13 former English colonies and those who wanted to maintain a confederation that would not challenge their sovereignty. However, with it, a state was born that could combine unity, necessary to prevent the re-emergence of conflicts between the old British colonies and to guarantee their protection externally, with autonomy, necessary for defending their own liberty. It was a state, which, as Alexander Hamilton (1787) said, "far from implying the abolition of state governments, makes them constituent parts of a sovereign nation, allowing them direct representation in the Senate and leaving a good part of sovereignty in their hands. This fully corresponds to the concept of a federal government in any possible and rational extension of the term." The federal model then spread worldwide, starting in the 20th century (except Switzerland, which became a federation in the 18th century), particularly in Commonwealth countries such as Australia, Canada, and India. In Latin America, Brazil and Nigeria, and Europe (besides Switzerland) and Germany adopted federal constitutions after World War II.

The main characteristic of the federal state is that, within it, the functional division of legislative, executive, and judicial powers is complemented by a territorial division of power between different levels of government that are simultaneously independent and coordinated.

In the existing federal states, two essential levels of government have been identified: the federal state and the member states. Unlike the situation in unitary states, in the federal state, the central government only has the minimum competences and power necessary to guarantee the political and economic unity of the federation, while the other levels are granted the capacity for self-governance in all other areas. This constitutional balance is also reflected in the composition of the legislative power, characterized by bicameralism. Using the example of existing federal states, part of the parliament represents the people of the federation based on the number of voters, while the other part consists of representatives of the states. To be passed, laws must achieve a majority vote from both the people's representatives and those from the member states. In the case of multiple levels of government, this type of bicameralism must be reproduced at each level. For the division of power between the central government and local governments to be guaranteed, it must be ratified by a written constitution but also protected by an autonomous power capable of annulling legislative and administrative provisions that do not comply with the constitution and ruling in the last instance on conflicts arising from the division of powers. This power is the judiciary, which bases its independence on the existence of different levels of government (each having an interest in safeguarding the judicial independence from other levels) and, thus, can guarantee the primacy of the constitution by ensuring that all federal state organs comply with it.

Finally, if no government authority should be subordinated to another in its areas of competence, each must have sufficient resources to develop the tasks entrusted by the constitution. Therefore, all levels must have the power to impose taxes for financing their services and policies.

Thus, what differentiates a federal state from a confederation is the existence of an authentic power that, on the one hand, can regulate relations between member states based on existing legislation and prevent the use of force in cases of conflicts or disputes, and, on the other hand, has direct power over citizens, who form the state democratically. In the vision of federalists, a confederation is not a state, but a sum of sovereign states that regulate their relations based on force as a last resort and retain exclusive power over their citizens. A confederation is based on the principle of state representation, not citizen representation, and grants voting rights only to states, thus excluding the people from decisions affecting interstate relations. The veto power, which is always included in confederations and can paralyse any common action by imposing the will of a single individual on the majority, is the symbol of the absolute sovereignty maintained by the states forming a confederation.

In conclusion, due to the mechanism of halving democratic representation and, therefore, thanks to the coexistence of the principle of unity of the political community and the independence of its parts, the federal state is able to balance the advantages of a small scale, which allows individuals to participate directly in the political decision-making process, with the advantages of a large scale, necessary to ensure security and economic development. Hamilton defines the essential character of this institutional innovation as the expansion of the democratic government framework from a state to a union of states, meaning the possibility of unifying different national communities and achieving political participation over an unlimited territorial extent. This means that the federal state is not only a new form of governance but also a new form of international organization, the only one capable of achieving complete peace, because it removes the power from states to start a war, transforming power relations into relationships based on law. By allowing citizens to participate democratically in the formation of the power that regulates relations between states, federal institutions achieve federal democracy. The federal state can only be fully realised in the context of world federalisation, and its historical manifestations have so far been imperfect and unstable.

In the federalist conception, global federalization is undoubtedly a long-term objective and the only perspective in which a positive and democratic response can be given to the growing global interdependence, which has transformed the world into a community of destinies, and to the crisis of nation-states, which are inadequate to face the great global challenges, whether they are economic, political, ecological, or even social and cultural. This explains why integration processes are underway in all parts of the world (European Union, NAFTA, Mercosur, Andean Pact, ASEAN, CIS, African regional unions, etc.), which, if deepened, will have only one destination – that of federalization; and Europe is the continent where this process is most advanced, and where awareness of the revolutionary significance of the transformation is greatest.

1.2. Functionalism

1.2.1. David Mitrany and Functionalism

Functionalism emerged as a response to the devastation of World War I, part of a broader intellectual movement seeking to theorise conditions for enduring peace. British sociologist **David Mitrany** became the principal architect of functionalist thought, advocating for a new international order grounded in transnational cooperation. Unlike approaches focused solely on regional integration, Mitrany envisioned a global system where cooperation would transcend national boundaries and evolve through practical, task-oriented collaboration. This vision is articulated in his seminal work, *A Working Peace System* (1943).

Functionalism is considered a foundational component of the institutional-liberal school of thought that gained momentum in the mid-1940s. His ideas were shaped by rationalist and reformist currents such as Fabianism, guild socialism, and syndicalism, which emphasised social progress through planned, collective action. This school of thought significantly influenced the development of international relations theory. Functionalism not only laid the groundwork for the neofunctionalist theory of regional integration but also inspired later approaches such as interdependence theory, regime theory, and world society theory.

Mitrany's core concern was the efficient management of resources as a precondition for sustainable international cooperation and long-term peace. His vision centred on fulfilling human needs and promoting public welfare over national prestige or ideology. He was critical of the nation-state's capacity to meet its citizens' needs, viewing it as a rigid and often obsolete framework.

In *The Progress of International Government* (1933), Mitrany urged the abandonment of what he called the "pagan worship of national borders" and proposed the creation of an international system based on functional agencies. These agencies would be entrusted with specific tasks and responsibilities, gradually assuming functions from nation-states. He envisioned a continuous transfer of authority from national governments to international institutions to better manage transboundary issues.

Thus, functionalism is considered the representative of the institutional-liberal school of thought that emerged in the mid-1940s with the publication of Mitrany's work *A Working Peace System*. His ideas were marked by radical-rationalist sentiments that found political expression in movements such as Fabianism, guild socialism, and even syndicalism in the UK.

This line of thought had a strong influence on the theory of international relations. Thus, functionalism is not only the intellectual precursor to the neofunctionalist theory of integration but also the starting point for recent approaches to the study of international relations, such as the theory of interdependence, the theory of regimes, and the theory of world society.

Mitrany's primary concern was the efficient management of limited resources as a premise for sustainable cooperation and for creating what he defined as "a working peace system." The central points of the functionalist agenda, as outlined by Mitrany, include prioritising human needs or public welfare and opposing the sanctity of the nation-state or the celebration of a particular political creed, extending to challenging the capacity of the nation-state to meet the people's needs. These two major components of his conception are the subject of two works that had a major impact on functionalist theory.

The first, *The Progress of International Government* (1933), advocates for states to abandon the "pagan worship of national borders." Instead, he proposes creating an international system of functional agencies in which there would be a continuous transfer of functions and authority from the jurisdiction of states to international bodies. In his second work, *A Working Peace System* (1943), Mitrany revisits the essential elements of the previous work. He begins with the assumption that some needs transcend national borders and that the existence of the state itself is nothing more than a fixed, inflexible framework that is unnecessary and hinders the realization of the public good, given that some needs can be better met by ignoring state borders. He believes that the primary rationale of national states' politics is the acquisition and retention of power, not the promotion of the public good. Ultimately, he concludes that the functionalist solution, based on fulfilling common tasks and the experience of cooperation that they require, meets the basic human demands for peace and social stability. Thus, the most beneficial in this regard are transnational institutions. They produce two effects: first, the transfer of loyalty to transnational institutions, and second, the reduction of international conflicts. Mitrany foresaw the proliferation of specialized international organizations as a means of responding to human needs, each dedicated to a specific domain and with a separate structure. He also envisioned endowing these internationally constituted functional organizations with the powers and resources necessary to carry out these functions. The result, according to Mitrany, would be a dense structure of government institutions with diverse and overlapping functions that would sustain the process of interdependence between states and societies. This could become a reality through agreements between one or more governments, allowing them to benefit from continuous cooperation in certain areas and the ongoing regulation of certain international activities. In this sense, the relocation of authority and resources from member states to these new international organizations is absolutely necessary. Nevertheless, he saw few differences between national states and federations as forms of international political organization, believing that federalism was merely an attempt to build regional arrangements for political purposes that would evolve, through social and radical transformations and planning, into a centralized, closed, exclusive system akin to states.

Thus, Mitrany remained firmly convinced of the superiority of the functionalist solution over the federalist one and the importance of global decentralisation over a regional approach to problems. In contrast to federalism, concerned with the final form of the integration process, functionalism believes that function determines form. This line of thought starts with the premise that people's needs change, so the form that the integration process will ultimately take must be flexible.

The functionalist approach has been criticised for idealism or naivety. Although Mitrany’s work focused primarily on identifying and explaining the dynamics of contemporary international relations, the question arose as to whether functionalism could be considered a theory of international relations or whether it should have been treated as a social theory. Functionalism, as proposed by David Mitrany, has been critiqued for its technocratic approach to complex political issues.

Mitrany's assumption that determining needs is an objective and technocratic exercise has been challenged, as it often overlooks the inherently political and competitive nature of such determinations. While functionalist models may be applicable in administrative areas like transportation, their application becomes more contentious in sectors such as production, trade, and distribution, which are deeply embedded in political and economic competition. (Popovici, 2010)

Critics argue that Mitrany's underestimation of the role of politics and his belief in the triumph of reason and technocracy over politics are overly idealistic and fail to account for the complexities of real-world governance. (Schmitterm, 2005) Generally, criticisms of Mitrany's theory can be grouped into three main categories:

- **Technocratic Bias and Underestimation of Politics**

Mitrany's focus on technical, task-oriented cooperation is criticised for underestimating the inherently political nature of international relations. Critics argue that functionalism's reliance on technocratic solutions ignores the power struggles, national interests, and competitive dynamics that shape global politics. According to scholars, functionalism presents an overly optimistic view of international cooperation, which neglects the importance of political negotiation and the role of state sovereignty (Popovici, 2010).

- **Limitations in Applying Functionalism to Economic and Political Spheres**

While functionalism works in areas like transportation, railways, or aviation, its application to sectors like trade, production, and distribution is much more difficult. These sectors are inherently competitive and politically charged, making it unrealistic to assume that international institutions could efficiently manage them without encountering resistance from powerful national interests. Critics point out that functionalism struggles in complex economic domains where competition among states is the driving force (Bickerton et al., 2014).

- **Over-Simplification of Sovereignty and the Role of the Nation-State**

Mitrany's theory is criticised for its oversimplification of the relationship between national sovereignty and international cooperation. Many argue that the continuous transfer of authority from nation-states to international institutions, as envisioned by Mitrany, is overly idealistic. The assumption that nation-states would willingly cede sovereignty is seen as unrealistic, as states are often reluctant to lose control over key aspects of governance, particularly in politically sensitive areas like security, trade, and foreign policy (Schmitter, 2005).

The inability to foresee the evolution of events has caused Mitrany’s work to be seen more as a plea than as an actual theory. Mitrany’s works could only be considered a theory if the intervention of politics is theorised and not if generalisations are intended.

It is unclear to what extent Mitrany’s belief in the prospect of positive changes in human behaviour can contribute to significant changes like international politics. There are no references to how needs are identified, no explanation of how actors come to share a common perception of the world, and there is no common set of hypotheses shared by all functionalists.

In these conditions, Mitrany's work hardly meets the rigorous standards required by the scientific approach to social sciences. Furthermore, Mitrany’s attempt to depoliticise international relations does not withstand the essential tests that any theory of international relations must undergo.

Mitrany's legacy in the debate surrounding European integration had both a theoretical and normative component. Starting from the limits of the nation-state, he became an advocate of a technocratic approach to what he perceived as the great issues of his time: the elimination of war and the establishment of world peace. His ideas became the starting point for other theories or approaches to international relations: neofunctionalism, the theory of interdependence, transnationalism, and governance without rulers. Neofunctionalists adapted the fundamental concepts of Mitrany’s theory, focusing on explaining the process of regional integration in Europe.

Unlike federalists, functionalists are more concerned with the importance of the integration process, which they see as a key factor in bringing about the change in the political order, than with the a priori description of its precise form or outcome. They observe the circumstances in which sectoral integration in specific political spheres may lead to what Mitrany defined as "a functional system to ensure peace" (*A Working Peace System*, 1943), paying little attention to the constitutional details that would involve transferring power and authority from the nation-state to supranational institutions.

A common point between the two supranational models is the vision of elites, although nuanced. Federalists view Europe as a major project that will only be realised through an agreement between elites and masses, with elites playing the role of mobilising the masses around the idea of change. Functionalists, however, believe that elites must lead this process, as they are the main agents of change. As Michael O'Neill stated, federalism proposes a radical "bottom-up" change, while functionalism proposes a gradual "top-down" change.

In this climate of opposition between federalism and functionalism as forms of supranational organisation for human activity and maintaining peace, the first major theory of integration emerged: neofunctionalism. The neofunctionalist project is closely tied to the strategies envisioned by the founders of the European Community. It emerged as a reaction against the idealism of the federalist movement, although the final outcome of the integration process could take a federal form. Thus, we generally speak of a federal model of the European Union's evolution, rather than a federal theory of European integration.

1.2.2. The Neofunctionalist Model of Ernst Haas

Neofunctionalism emerged as a response from a group of American scholars to what they perceived as the inadequacies of earlier theories in explaining or predicting developments on the international stage. These researchers emphasised methodological rigour and analytical depth rather than normative or prescriptive approaches.

Rooted in the behavioural revolution that transformed American political science in the 1960s, neofunctionalism shifted the focus of research from formal institutional frameworks to the behavior of political actors and the dynamic processes underpinning integration. This approach consciously distanced itself from constitutional or institutional models and instead emphasized empirical analysis of political behavior and system change.

In the neofunctionalist understanding of European integration, the starting point is the recognition that nation-states often perpetuate social and cultural divisions rooted in historical constructs. However, as modern governance demands evolve, these same nation-states struggle to meet the complex needs of their societies, gradually diminishing their primacy as the sole loci of authority. Like classical functionalists, neofunctionalists highlight the centrality of economic cooperation and welfare imperatives as drivers of integration. But they go further by emphasising the interplay of actors and the political dynamics that emerge through transnational collaboration.

Ernst B. Haas, the primary architect of neofunctionalism, conceptualised a supranational political entity as a progression beyond the traditional nation-state. His vision of regional governance resembled that of a modern, industrialised state, surpassing traditional models of intergovernmental cooperation, such as confederations or federations. For Haas, supranational integration offered a more advanced and adaptive model of governance suitable for pluralistic societies. In his major work on

European integration, *The Uniting of Europe: Political, Social*, Haas argues that the integration process goes beyond mere economic cooperation, suggesting that political integration is driven by the functional needs and spillover effects of cooperation. This book outlines the foundations of neofunctionalism, with a particular focus on the role of supranational institutions in advancing European unity.

Key elements of the neofunctionalist model include:

- **Spill-over**: One of the central mechanisms in Haas's theory, spill-over refers to the process by which integration in one sector (typically economic) creates pressures for integration in related sectors. This "functional spill-over" explains how the creation of the European Coal and Steel Community (ECSC) set the stage for further integration, eventually leading to the European Monetary Union. However, Haas emphasized that spill-over is not automatic; it requires coordination and guidance by a supranational authority. Drawing inspiration from Jean Monnet's vision of a centralized planning body akin to the French *Commissariat au Plan*, Haas asserted that clear, impactful objectives were necessary for integration to resonate with ordinary citizens and sustain momentum. The concept of spill-over became a cornerstone variable in the neofunctionalist theory, offering both inertia and dynamism to the process of regional integration.
- **Transfer of loyalty**: Another crucial concept in Haas's model, the transfer of loyalty refers to the gradual reorientation of political allegiance and activity from national institutions to newly formed supranational entities. As regional institutions demonstrate their capacity to address citizens' needs more effectively, political actors—including elites, interest groups, and eventually the public—begin to shift their support toward the new centres of authority. For neofunctionalists, understanding the mechanisms that facilitate this transfer is central to explaining the political dimension of integration.

Despite its analytical contributions, neofunctionalism has faced considerable criticism. Scholars have questioned the model's implicit assumption of linear and irreversible progress, arguing that integration does not follow a uniformly upward trajectory. Indeed, the rise of nationalism within the European Community during the 1960s—exemplified by Charles de Gaulle's opposition to supranational authority—challenged the technocratic and apolitical assumptions of neofunctionalism.

Critics, most notably Stanley Hoffmann, contended that neofunctionalism underestimated the enduring power of nation-states and the central role they continue to play in safeguarding fundamental values such as liberty, justice, and sovereignty. Hoffmann's intergovernmentalist approach emerged as a paradigmatic counterpoint to Haas's neofunctionalist thesis, emphasising the primacy of national interests and state-centric decision-making.

Confronted with the resurgence of nationalism and the stagnation of the integration process in the 1970s, Haas himself revisited and revised his theoretical stance. In an acid 1971 article, he acknowledged the limitations of his model, particularly its overreliance on the specific historical and political conditions of postwar Western Europe. He recognised that neofunctionalism, grounded in the context of pluralist, industrialised societies, might not be universally applicable, especially to integration efforts in non-European or less economically developed regions. Additionally, Haas admitted that the theory lacked a clear articulation of an endpoint or ultimate goal for the European integration process.

1.2.3. Jean Monnet and His Contribution to Functionalism

Jean Monnet, one of the founding fathers of European integration, is widely recognised for his practical application of functionalist principles to postwar European reconstruction and political cooperation. Though not a theorist in the academic sense, Monnet's work laid the foundation for functionalism as an operational strategy and profoundly influenced both the theory and practice of regional integration.

Monnet believed that lasting peace and prosperity in Europe could not be achieved through traditional diplomacy or by attempting to negotiate comprehensive political agreements from the outset. Instead, he advocated for a pragmatic and incremental approach—cooperation in specific functional sectors, particularly economic ones—that would generate tangible benefits and, over time, lead to deeper political integration. This method, often described as *"functional integration by stealth"* (Majone, 1995), reflected a deep understanding of institutional evolution and political behaviour in divided societies.

His most notable achievement was the creation of the **European Coal and Steel Community (ECSC)** in 1951, a supranational organization that regulated coal and steel production among six European countries. The ECSC represented the first concrete step toward institutionalized European unity. By placing these two critical industries, central to military capability, under common management, Monnet aimed to make future wars between France and Germany not only unthinkable but materially impossible.

Monnet's approach can be seen as the embodiment of **functionalism in practice**. He argued that cooperation in technical and economic areas would build trust and interdependence among states, gradually expanding to other domains through a process of **spill-over**, whereby integration in one sector would naturally necessitate cooperation in others. Over time, the supranational institutions created to manage these sectors would acquire greater authority and legitimacy, ultimately contributing to the formation of a broader political community.

A core element of Monnet's vision was the **creation of strong, independent institutions** that could act in the collective European interest. He believed that integration should be driven by institutions with real powers, capable of implementing decisions and shaping policy. For this reason, he played a central role in designing the ECSC's **High Authority**, the forerunner of today's European Commission, with competencies that went well beyond those of a traditional international organisation.

Monnet also recognised the importance of **elite consensus and technocratic governance**. He believed that political elites and experts should guide integration, as they possessed the knowledge and foresight needed to make decisions in the long-term public interest. Public support would follow as citizens experienced the concrete benefits of integration in their daily lives. This **top-down model** of integration aligned closely with the assumptions of both classical functionalism and neofunctionalism.

Monnet's idea regarding the European Community consisted of a combination of functionalist principles, with the ultimate goal being the creation of a federal government. For Monnet, federalism was merely the culmination of a long and complex process that involved the gradual modification of conventional perceptions of international cooperation (rather than directly confronting them, as most federalists were tempted to do). The strategy developed by Monnet for constructing European unity can be defined as a gradualist or functionalist method.

Jean Monnet placed great importance on institutions in determining the future form of European integration. He, along with Robert Schuman, formulated the plan that led to the establishment of the European Coal and Steel Community: "The Community we created is not an end in itself. It is a process of change… It is impossible to predict today the decisions that should be made in a new context tomorrow. The most important thing is not to abandon the few principles that have guided us from the beginning: the creation of a common interest among Europeans, which is served by common democratic institutions to which sovereignty has been delegated. This is the dynamic that has never ceased to operate... I have never doubted that one day this process will lead us to the United States of Europe, but it makes no sense to try to imagine today the political form it will take" (Monnet, 1978). Europe is to be formed of "nations that commit themselves without temporal limits and without looking back." (Monnet, 1978)

The interdependence of sectors in the modern economy creates technical pressures for the expansion of the number of sectors transferred to the supranational level. This functional spill-over process starts with basic economic sectors (agriculture and trade) and targets higher sectors like the single market, monetary policy, and foreign and security policy, supported by supranational institutions that will develop over time (political spill-over).

Thus, integration based on the "Monnet Method" represents an ongoing process that leads to the achievement of the major goal: the creation of a European federation (a union of autonomous states, maintaining their independence within certain limits, in a unitary state governed by a central government).

According to neofunctionalism, the recipe for a progressively closer Union is as follows:

- Integration will begin in sectors of low politics, but these must be strategically significant economically.
- A "High" authority (composed of technocrats) will be created to oversee the integration process.
- **Spill-over I**: Integration of specific sectors of the national economy will create functional pressures for integrating other interdependent sectors. The "High Authority" will direct these developments (ECSC – EEC – EMU).
- **Spill-over II**: National interest groups will transfer their loyalties and lobbying activities to the new center. The functional method only describes the formation of a union; it does not show how the optimal framework for identities and the sense of loyalty supporting such an evolution should be realized. The behavior of those involved is primarily determined by their self-interests, mostly economic in nature.

Despite his successes, Monnet's approach was not without critics. Some argued that the technocratic and incremental nature of his strategy lacked democratic legitimacy and transparency. Others viewed the strategy of avoiding politically sensitive issues, such as national sovereignty or constitutional reform, as insufficient for building a truly united Europe. Nevertheless, Monnet remained committed to the idea that functional cooperation would gradually transform Europe's political landscape and reduce the relevance of national boundaries.

In summary, Jean Monnet's contribution to functionalism was not theoretical but profoundly **strategic and institutional**. He operationalised functionalist principles in a way that transformed them from abstract ideas into effective mechanisms for integration. His vision of step-by-step cooperation through common institutions laid the groundwork for the European Economic Community and, ultimately, the European Union. Today, many of the core elements of EU governance, including sectoral integration, the role of supranational institutions, and the process of incremental political consolidation, bear the imprint of Monnet's functionalist legacy.

Although there is no doubt about the importance of Jean Monnet's contribution to the development of the Community, his placement within one of the two supranational currents remains a subject of debate.

1.3. Intergovernmentalism

Supporters of intergovernmentalism emphasise nation-states and sovereignty. Since political action is grounded in power and the struggle between conflicting interests, according to intergovernmentalist or state-centric theory, the integration process develops as far as the state allows. Member states, by relinquishing part of their national sovereignty, aim to establish an institutional framework that ensures this transfer of sovereignty while keeping the decision-making power in the hands of the nation-state. In European studies, the realist current has taken the form of intergovernmentalism, although it cannot be said that the two schools of thought overlap perfectly.

The starting point of intergovernmental theories is the crisis triggered by French President General de Gaulle, the most prominent representative of Western European nationalism at that time in the community system, and the solution through which the member countries decided to end this crisis.

The 1965 crisis emerged against the backdrop of attempts by the European Commission, led by Walter Hallstein, to extend supranational principles at the expense of national sovereignty. The 1965 dispute represented the culmination of older divergences between two opposed European conceptions: that of France's partners (who favored a supranational structure) and that of General de Gaulle, who advocated for a “Europe of the Nations” (opposed to the extension of supranational principles at the expense of national sovereignty). After the 1965-1966 crisis and until the early 1990s, intergovernmentalism dominated the practice and intellectual discourse in European studies.

Proponents of intergovernmentalism place primary emphasis on nation-states and the preservation of sovereignty. In this view, since political action is inherently grounded in power dynamics and conflicts of interest, the process of European integration can only advance to the extent that individual states permit it. By voluntarily relinquishing certain aspects of national sovereignty, member states aim to construct an institutional framework that enables this limited transfer of authority while ensuring that ultimate decision-making power remains with national governments.

In European studies, intergovernmentalism draws intellectual inspiration from the realist tradition in international relations. Although the two are not identical, realism and intergovernmentalism share foundational assumptions about the primacy of the state in international politics.

According to intergovernmentalist theory, the integration process is largely driven by national interests and domestic political considerations. Member states transfer authority to supranational bodies only when the anticipated benefits outweigh the costs, particularly for short-term political gains or in response to technical policy needs. Supranational institutions, while facilitating cooperation, are understood to be agents of the member states, constrained by mandates defined at intergovernmental summits, particularly by the European Council.

Intergovernmentalism rests on several key assumptions:

- National sovereignty remains the cornerstone of political authority, even if it is exercised jointly within the EU framework.
- National governments are the central actors in shaping European outcomes, with supranational institutions playing a secondary role.
- Economic integration does not necessarily lead to political integration, challenging neofunctionalist assumptions.
- National interest and high politics will ultimately prevail over technocratic or ideological agendas.

- National identities and loyalties are resilient and resistant to supranational transformation.

This state-centric model has been criticised for setting preferences and goals to states without explaining how these preferences are formed or how complex institutional settings shape decision-makers' beliefs.

The most influential and nuanced exposition of intergovernmentalism came from political scientist **Stanley Hoffmann**. In seminal works such as "*The European Process at Atlantic Crosspurposes*" (1964) and *"Obstinate or Obsolete?"* (1966), Hoffmann challenged neofunctionalist claims that European integration would inevitably erode national sovereignty. He argued that the unique cultural, historical, and political diversity of Europe rendered the creation of a political union, modelled after the United States, both unlikely and unrealistic.

For Hoffmann, the endurance of the nation-state was not a sign of obsolescence but rather a reflection of its adaptive capacity. European integration, in his view, did not replace the nation-state but instead allowed it to survive in a changing global context. He acknowledged that integration could occur in domains of "low politics"—such as trade, transportation, or agriculture, where stakes were lower. However, in "high politics" defence, foreign affairs, and sovereignty, states would remain the dominant actors. Hoffmann was sceptical of attempts to bypass national authority through supranational technocratic governance, warning against illusions of elite-driven, ideologically neutral integration.

Yet even Hoffmann agreed that some form of federal organisation could offer Europe its best chance at effectiveness, not as a break from the nation-state, but as an extension of it. He famously wrote: "Europe cannot be what some of its nations were, a people creating their state, nor can it be what some of the oldest states on the continent aspire to be, a people created by the state. Europe must wait until its peoples feel close enough to justify creating a state to unite them."

Despite Hoffmann's insights, intergovernmentalism has been challenged on several fronts:

1. The rigid separation between "low" and "high" politics appears increasingly artificial, as issues like migration, climate change, and digital security blur traditional boundaries.
2. The assumption that national sovereignty is impermeable is outdated in a context of deep global interdependence.

3. The notion that states have retained their full autonomy ignores how globalisation and Europeanization have limited their capacity to act unilaterally.
4. Hoffmann's interpretation of the setbacks in the integration process in the 1960s and 1970s may have been overly pessimistic, failing to anticipate later developments like the Single European Act and the Maastricht Treaty.

Nevertheless, intergovernmentalism has made a valuable contribution by emphasising the role of states in maintaining legitimacy and political accountability. The oil shocks, currency instability, and global realignments of the 1970s reinforced the need for coordinated intergovernmental responses. This pragmatic cooperation gradually evolved toward a confederal model of integration.

While states remain central actors in the EU, their authority is no longer absolute or monolithic. The intergovernmentalist model increasingly coexists with newer approaches that account for hybrid governance, multilevel politics, and the complex interplay of national and supranational forces. In response to its limitations, intergovernmentalism has evolved. Theories such as liberal intergovernmentalism and new institutionalist frameworks have sought to refine the model. At the same time, scholars have employed political science and international relations tools to study integration as a hybrid process, one shaped by both domestic political dynamics and institutional structures at the European level.

This shift reflects a broader understanding that integration outcomes are not dictated solely by state preferences but are the result of strategic interactions among multiple actors across different governance levels.

2. Current Trends in the European Integration Process

2.1. Regional Interdependence

Regional interdependence is a theoretical approach in which the European Union is identified as a response to a "cascade interdependence" with implications both on domestic politics and international politics. While the intergovernmental model has influenced this approach, states are viewed differently, being forced to share many traditional competencies with actors from within, outside, and above them. As a result, the role of states in the governance of the European Union and integration is no longer the central subject of this theory. On the other hand, this theoretical conception aligns with the principles of supranational theories, more specifically with the functionalist branch, due to its focus on informal links and political relations, as well as prioritising the process over the institutions. This leads to the situation where domestic politics shape regional processes, and the international environment influences the regional process, exerting a strong influence on the domestic political environment of states.

The outcome is the replacement of the borders between the internal or national and regional or international spheres with more fluid transactional flows between various levels and institutions within the European Union. Considering the role given to these transactional flows, this conception comes close again to functionalism, but without the determinism that led Haas to overstate his argument: negotiations stimulate a broad range of transactional relations, but they do not necessarily suggest a clear inertia to sustain the integration process. In other words, close cooperation does not guarantee the articulation of common interests; rather, it can have different consequences depending on the issue at hand: forging alliances or generating hostilities. Conceptualizing the regional process as a source of transnational cooperation and intergovernmental discord is far from the realistic notion of the state as a political organization capable of enacting laws and enforcing them within a territory.

Applied to the study of the European Union, this approach does not seem to confirm intergovernmental, confederal, or supranational predictions, but instead focuses on the dynamics of global change.

Since it does not fit into any of the classical paradigms but seeks to synthesize them, overcoming their shortcomings to arrive at an intrinsic approach to international relations, this approach has gained considerable success in recent years. From this perspective, the European Union is seen as a political entity that finds its place in a broader globalisation process, possessing sophisticated procedures, rules, and a vast institutional network in which states must compete for advantages or minimise risks through highly elaborate arrangements.

2.2. Confederalism

This theoretical approach emerged as an attempt to correct the shortcomings of the classic intergovernmental model proposed by Hoffmann. Viewing the European Union as a complex political space, confederalism focuses on the Union's intermediary status between an international regime or federation and a republican political entity. The European Union is thus suspended between intergovernmentalism and supranationalism, between recognizing the need for more effective common action and the inability of states to concentrate their actions or cede their own authority.

A confederation is considered a voluntary association of sovereign states with common interests. It involves interstate arrangements governed by the same principles as those that govern their international politics, while each member state retains its sovereign right to decide on its foreign policy. In general, the confederation solution has been considered one of the three alternatives available to states to maximize and streamline their process of promoting their interests internationally while maintaining their sovereign attributes (the other two being the exercise of hegemony and influencing the balance of power) by facilitating practical cooperation means, creating institutional mechanisms beyond diplomatic ones, devising rules and procedures to minimize the risk of conflict, strengthening cooperation capabilities among member states, and creating conditions for a stable social order. Institutionalizing relations between countries within the group is necessary to ensure the durability and stability of the system.

Confederalism can provide several explanations for the tension arising from the interaction between governments promoting national interests and supranational actors challenging the boundaries of traditional politics. Over time, confederalism has taken on many forms in the literature: union of states, condominium, confederation, and consociation. The latter has received particular attention, especially after the publication of works on the topic by sociologist A. Lijphardt, who tried to explain how strongly divided societies can achieve internal political stability by building judicial institutions and a consensual political culture among elites.

The main proponents of this line of thought, such as P. Taylor, D. Crysschoon, and W. Wallace, tend towards a cautious interpretation, emphasising the resistance of governments to the expansion of supranational institutions' interference with traditional prerogatives. For instance, minimal gains concerning transparency in the Council or overcoming the democratic deficit, the ambiguity surrounding the final trajectory of the European Union, and the contradictory government agendas that impose sensitive negotiations are often cited. In conclusion, states retain control over the European project, and the European political entity is shaped by persistent national interests, even though these are promoted through transnational procedures. This approach sets the stage for a shift, identifying tensions between divergent aspirations toward integration as a modus vivendi of the project. The emphasis is on negotiations to reconcile diverse interests, rather than on attempting political harmonisation or creating a common identity. In another vision, confederalism could be a step toward the creation of a federal Europe or an attempt to refine the intergovernmental model to make it adaptable to the conditions of globalisation.

What is generally criticised in this theoretical approach is its tendency to focus more on institutions than on structures and functions. The model remains deficient in explaining the political status of the Union or the dynamics of the regional integration process.

2.3. Multi-level Governance

Since neither of the two major integration theories (supranationalism and intergovernmentalism) corresponds to the modern nation-state and the European Union, a new theory emerges: multi-level governance.

The assumptions on which this approach is based are the following:

- Decision-making competencies are distributed across multiple levels and are no longer the monopoly of government. National governments have an important decision-making role, but control shifts to the supranational level. Furthermore, national governments are no longer able to control the mobilisation of subnational interests on the European stage. National sovereignty has an independent role that does not derive from the agents of national governments.
- The common decisions of the governments of the member states of the European Union lead to the loss of control by national governments, with qualified

majority voting playing an increasingly important role in the decision-making process;

- "Political arenas" are interconnected; supranational and subnational actors operate in combination.

The "state-centric" concepts used to describe modern states are already outdated due to the disappearance of distinctions between state and society, between national and international. Thus, the distinction between state/society is no longer so prominent because in negotiations about the interests of a country, at the local, regional, or national level, not only governments participate, but also private actors (transnational companies, interest groups) and civil society represented by non-governmental organisations. The modern state increasingly resembles not a hierarchical structure of legitimate authority but a system of negotiation at various levels, in which public actors are not unnecessary, but can function efficiently only by cooperating with private actors and other groups.

Even the distinction between national/international loses its significance, as the traditional division between domestic and international affairs becomes redundant in the days of globalization and Europeanization, carried out according to rules established by certain international authorities (such as the WTO, for example).

Approaching the European Union as a multi-level political entity avoids overemphasizing the state and treats the Union as an entity that operates not only at the European level through its established institutions. From this perspective, authority is dispersed among the actors of the European political stage (not just states), placed at various levels. Their competencies overlap significantly, and interactions occur simultaneously at multiple levels, suggesting the complexity of governing such a political entity.

3. The European Union After 2006: Integration and Fragmentation

Since 2006, the European Union (EU) has undergone substantial transformation, marked by significant advancements in integration and institutional reforms, as well as rising fragmentation.

A combination of internal reforms, economic crises, external challenges, and the evolving global geopolitical landscape has defined this period. These developments have had profound implications for the EU's institutional structure, policy direction, and global role. Despite the progress made in areas like economic governance and climate policy, the EU has also faced increasing fragmentation, which has undermined its unity in certain domains.

3.1. Institutional Reforms and Strengthened Integratio

A crucial moment in the EU's institutional evolution occurred with the **Treaty of Lisbon**, signed in 2007 and effective as of December 1, 2009, which marked a landmark in the development of European integration. Intended to replace the failed Constitutional Treaty, the Lisbon Treaty aimed to streamline EU operations and enhance its democratic legitimacy. This treaty was designed to address inefficiencies in the EU's decision-making processes, increase transparency, and provide greater legitimacy to the Union's actions. The treaty introduced several important institutional reforms that reshaped the governance of the EU:

1. **Creation of the Permanent President of the European Council**: Before the Lisbon Treaty, the presidency of the European Council rotated every six months among member states. The creation of a permanent president aimed to ensure more continuity in leadership and a stronger presence in EU external relations. This role was first filled by **Herman Van Rompuy**, and later by **Charles Michel**. The permanent presidency helped to consolidate the EU's external representation, making the Union more coherent in its foreign policy (European Union Law).
2. **Increased Powers for the European Parliament**: The Lisbon Treaty granted the European Parliament more legislative authority, especially in areas such as trade, agriculture, and immigration. The Parliament became a co-legislator alongside the Council of the EU, allowing it to share legislative powers in more

policy domains, making EU laws more democratic and responsive to citizens' concerns (European Parliament Research Service).

3. **The High Representative for Foreign Affairs and Security Policy**: The treaty also established the position of the High Representative, merging the roles of the EU foreign policy chief and the European Commissioner for External Relations. The goal was to streamline the EU's foreign policy and make it more coherent. The High Representative, first held by **Catherine Ashton** and later by **Federica Mogherini**, is responsible for representing the EU in international negotiations and managing the EU's diplomatic and security affairs (European External Action Service).

These institutional reforms were meant to make the EU more efficient and capable of addressing the complex challenges of the 21st century. However, while these changes enhanced the EU's decision-making capacity, they also exposed some vulnerabilities in the Union's internal cohesion, particularly when it came to achieving consensus among member states with diverging interests. These institutional upgrades aligned with supranationalist thinking by strengthening the role of EU-level actors while retaining intergovernmental controls, especially in sensitive areas like foreign policy.

3.2. Policy Advancements and Deeper Integration

Several policy areas witnessed significant advancements in integration during this period, with the EU positioning itself as a global actor in areas such as climate change, economic governance, and enlargement.

1. **Climate Policy and the European Green Deal**: One of the EU's most ambitious policy initiatives in recent years has been the **European Green Deal**, unveiled in December 2019. The Green Deal aims to make Europe the world's first climate-neutral continent by 2050, a goal that includes reducing greenhouse gas emissions, promoting the use of renewable energy, and improving energy efficiency across member states. The Green Deal has sparked a wide-ranging shift toward green investment, with policies promoting clean energy, biodiversity preservation, and carbon reduction (European Commission).
2. **Economic Governance and the European Semester**: In the aftermath of the 2008 global financial crisis, the EU implemented a series of economic reforms to strengthen fiscal discipline and prevent future crises. The **European Semester**, introduced in 2010, is a framework for coordinating economic policies across member states. It allows the EU to review national budgets,

monitor fiscal compliance, and provide recommendations for economic reform. This process was designed to ensure that member states adhere to EU rules, particularly those relating to budget deficits and public debt (European Commission Economic Governance).

3. **EU Enlargement**: In 2007, the EU expanded to include **Bulgaria and Romania**, further solidifying its influence in Eastern Europe. These additions were part of the EU's ongoing commitment to promoting stability and democratic governance in the region. The enlargement process slowed in the subsequent years, but the EU continued to offer membership prospects to Western Balkan countries, including Serbia, Montenegro, and North Macedonia. Enlargement has played a crucial role in spreading European values, including democracy, human rights, and the rule of law (european-union.europa.eu).

3.3. Emerging Fragmentation: Challenges to Unity

Despite these efforts at deepening integration, the EU has faced significant challenges that have led to fragmentation in certain areas. These challenges often arise from diverging political, economic, and social priorities across member states, as well as growing populist and eurosceptic movements.

1. **Internal Market Fragmentation**: While the EU's internal market remains a fundamental pillar of the Union, it has struggled to fully harmonise services, digital markets, and taxation across member states. For example, digital services are subject to varying regulations across different countries, which hampers cross-border innovation and trade. Similarly, differences in national tax policies and labour laws have led to uneven economic outcomes across the EU, weakening the cohesiveness of the internal market and hindering economic growth (ecipe.org, ecipe.org).
2. **Political Polarization and Euroscepticism**: Euroscepticism has risen significantly in recent years, particularly in countries such as Hungary, Poland, and the United Kingdom. The 2016 Brexit referendum, which led to the UK's decision to leave the EU, was a dramatic manifestation of this trend. The rise of far-right and nationalist parties in many EU member states has further complicated the EU's ability to forge consensus on key issues such as immigration, the rule of law, and economic governance. This political fragmentation has at times made it difficult for the EU to present a unified stance on important issues (lemonde.fr, wsj.com).

3. **Geopolitical Fragmentation**: The EU's ability to act as a cohesive geopolitical actor has also been tested by external challenges. The conflict in Ukraine, for example, has exposed divisions among member states regarding the EU's response to Russia's aggression. While some countries, like Poland and the Baltic States, have advocated for a strong, united EU response, others have been more cautious. These differences reflect deeper divisions within the EU regarding issues of defense, foreign policy, and strategic autonomy. The EU's inconsistent response to the crisis has highlighted the challenge of maintaining a unified external policy in an increasingly multipolar world (link.springer.com).

3.4. Migration, Border Management, and Solidarity in the European Union

The **migration crisis of 2015** brought significant challenges to the European Union (EU), testing the limits of its solidarity mechanisms and determining separation between member states over how to handle the flow of refugees and migrants. The crisis, which saw a dramatic increase in the number of people fleeing conflicts and instability, particularly from Syria, Afghanistan, and Iraq, highlighted the vulnerabilities of the EU's internal mechanisms for managing migration and border control. It also provoked the tension between the EU's commitment to human rights and its political and economic interests, as well as between national sovereignty and supranational governance (European Parliament Research Service, 2020).

3.4.1. The Dublin Regulation and the Crisis of Shared Responsibility

The **Dublin Regulation**, a milestone of the EU's asylum policy, states that the first EU country of entry is responsible for processing asylum claims. Under this framework, asylum seekers were expected to be registered and processed in the country they first arrived in, and once their claim was processed, they could remain in that country or face deportation to their initial point of entry if they moved to another state (Frontex, 2020).

However, the **2015 migration crisis** exposed significant flaws in the Dublin system. Countries like **Italy**, **Greece**, and **Hungary**, which were the main points of entry for migrants coming to the EU, were overwhelmed by the sheer number of arrivals. These countries faced logistical challenges in processing asylum claims and political and social challenges as they struggled to integrate large numbers of refugees into their economies and societies.

At the same time, countries in **Northern Europe** and **Western Europe**, such as **Germany**, **Sweden**, and **Austria**, which had more developed economies and stronger social welfare systems, were seen as more attractive destinations for migrants. However, their ability to accept such a large number of migrants was constrained by both domestic political opposition and the limits of the Dublin Regulation. As a result, these countries began to push for **reforms to the Dublin system** that would allow for the more equitable distribution of asylum seekers across the EU (BBC News, 2020).

3.4.2. Divisions in the EU: National Sovereignty vs. Shared Responsibility

The **migration crisis** highlighted the **deep divisions** within the EU over how to address migration and asylum issues. The proposal for a **quota-based relocation scheme**, which would distribute asylum seekers across the EU based on each member state's capacity and population, was met with strong resistance from several Eastern and Central European countries, including **Hungary**, **Poland**, **Slovakia**, and the **Czech Republic**. These countries argued that imposing a quota system infringed upon their national sovereignty and that they should have the right to determine their own immigration policies (Migration Watch UK, 2015).

At the same time, **Germany** and **France**, two of the EU's largest and most influential members, supported the relocation scheme, arguing that shared responsibility was the only way to ensure that the EU could manage migration effectively and humanely. This division between **intergovernmental** approaches, where countries prioritise their own national interests, and **supranational** approaches, where countries agree to shared governance and solidarity, was one of the most visible tensions of the crisis.

The resistance to shared responsibility also reflected a **reassertion of national sovereignty** in border control and asylum policy. Countries with more restrictive immigration policies, such as Hungary, began to strengthen their borders, constructing physical barriers and implementing stricter controls on asylum seekers. This trend revived **intergovernmentalist arguments** about the primacy of nation-states in high politics, as national governments became increasingly unwilling to cede authority over their borders to EU institutions (European Commission, 2020).

3.4.3. The Long-Term Impact of the Migration Crisis on EU Solidarity

The **2015 migration crisis** and the challenges it created for EU migration policy have had a profound impact on the **EU's concept of solidarity**. The crisis exposed the limits of the EU's traditional solidarity mechanisms and raised questions about the future of European integration in the face of migration challenges.

While the EU was able to implement some reforms, such as strengthening **Frontex** and pursuing the **New Pact on Migration and Asylum**, the divisions between member states over how to manage migration persist.

For some EU countries, the migration crisis reinforced the idea that national governments must maintain control over their borders and asylum policies. For others, it demonstrated the need for a more **cohesive and collective approach**, where all EU countries share responsibility for asylum seekers and refugees. As the EU continues to grapple with migration challenges, the balance between national sovereignty and supranational governance will remain a key issue for the future of the Union's migration policy.

To conclude, the migration crisis of 2015 underscored the tensions between national sovereignty and EU solidarity, particularly in the context of migration and border management. While some EU countries advocated for a more cooperative and shared approach, others prioritised their national interests and resisted the EU's attempts to redistribute responsibility for asylum seekers. The crisis revealed the difficulties of achieving solidarity in an increasingly fragmented Europe, where member states have divergent priorities and political pressures.

However, the EU's response to the crisis, particularly in strengthening **Frontex** and reforming the migration and asylum system, has shown that supranational responses can be implemented, even in the face of resistance. The future of EU migration policy will depend on finding a delicate balance between national sovereignty and shared responsibility, ensuring that all member states contribute to a collective solution while respecting their individual concerns. As migration continues to be a key issue on the EU agenda, the EU will need to evolve and adapt its policies to better manage the challenges posed by migration, border control, and asylum.

3.5. Brexit: Disintegration Amid Integration

The United Kingdom's departure from the EU (Brexit) in 2020 represented the first major instance of EU disintegration. Driven by concerns over sovereignty, immigration, and the perceived overreach of EU institutions, Brexit revived nationalist discourses.

Yet paradoxically, Brexit also reinforced integrationist momentum among remaining members. The EU displayed unprecedented unity during withdrawal negotiations and emphasized cohesion post-Brexit, resulting in deeper cooperation in several areas, including defense and health policy.

The **Brexit** referendum, held on June 23, 2016, marked a historical moment for the European Union (EU). The United Kingdom's decision to leave the EU was, besides a political shock, a symbolic fracture in the process of European integration. While the EU has long sought deeper integration, Brexit revealed the tension between political unity and national sovereignty and the incurred challenges of balancing diverse member-state interests.

3.5.1. Historical Context and Causes of Brexit

Brexit cannot be understood without considering the historical context of the UK's relationship with the EU. The UK joined the European Economic Community (EEC) in 1973, after initially rejecting membership in the 1950s. However, the UK's relationship with the EEC and later the EU was often marked by scepticism and ambivalence. The UK participated in the Single Market but opted out of key EU policies such as the Economic and Monetary Union (EMU) and the Schengen Area. This "half-in, half-out" approach fostered a sense of detachment from deeper EU integration, which was further exacerbated by a growing Eurosceptic sentiment within British political life.

Several factors contributed to the decision to leave the EU:

1. **Sovereignty Concerns**: A significant part of the Brexit argument revolved around the perceived erosion of national sovereignty. Many British citizens and politicians felt that EU membership undermined the UK's ability to govern itself, particularly in areas like immigration, trade policy, and judicial authority. Eurosceptics argued that the UK was being forced to comply with EU

regulations and decisions, many of which they viewed as contrary to British interests and values (Wyn Jones, R. & T. Houghton, 2019).

2. **Immigration**: Immigration was another major issue that motivated Brexit supporters. The free movement of people within the EU meant that citizens of other EU countries could live and work in the UK, leading to significant demographic changes. Some Britons were concerned about the pressure on public services, housing, and jobs, and there was a perception that the UK's borders were too porous. The arrival of refugees and migrants from the EU, particularly from Eastern Europe, further fueled these concerns (Migration Observatory, 2020).
3. **Economic Discontent**: Economic factors also played a role in the Brexit decision. While the UK benefitted from access to the EU's single market, there were concerns over the EU's regulatory burden, its trade policies, and the contributions the UK was making to the EU budget. The EU's financial regulations and bureaucratic processes were seen by some as a drag on economic growth, particularly for small businesses and sectors that relied on external markets (Economic and Social Research Council).

3.5.2. The Economic and Institutional Impact of Brexit

Brexit has had deep consequences for both the UK and the EU. Economically, the UK's decision to leave the EU has created uncertainty in relation to trade, investment, and labour mobility.

1. **Trade and Economic Integration**: One of the key consequences of Brexit has been the disruption of the UK's trade relations with the EU. As a member of the EU, the UK benefitted from tariff-free access to the EU's single market, the largest trading bloc in the world. Upon leaving, the UK faced new trade barriers, including customs checks, regulatory divergence, and restrictions on the free movement of goods and services. As a result, the UK's exports to the EU have fallen, and businesses have faced higher costs and delays at the border (House of Commons Library, 2020).
2. **Labor Mobility and Immigration**: The end of free movement has also had a significant impact on labor markets in both the UK and the EU. In the UK, industries such as agriculture, healthcare, and hospitality, which heavily relied on EU migrant labor, have struggled to fill vacancies. Similarly, the EU has faced challenges in filling positions in sectors that previously relied on British

workers, particularly in areas like finance and professional services. The movement of people between the UK and EU countries has slowed considerably (Migration Watch UK).

3. **Institutional Impact on the EU**: While Brexit removed one of the EU's major powers, it also presented the EU with challenges regarding its internal cohesion and the future direction of integration. The departure of the UK, one of the EU's largest economies, created a gap in the Union's political and economic structure. It raised questions about the future of the EU's budget and policies, particularly in areas like defense, economic policy, and international trade. However, Brexit also provided an opportunity for the EU to deepen integration among the remaining member states, particularly in areas like economic governance and foreign policy. The EU has sought to use Brexit as an impetus for reform and to strengthen its political and economic bonds (European Council on Foreign Relations).

3.5.3. Brexit and the Future of European Integration

Brexit represents a paradox: a disintegration in a period of otherwise advancing European integration. It has brought to the forefront the tension between the EU's goals of deeper political and economic union and the sovereignty concerns of individual member states. While the EU has continued to push forward with initiatives like the **European Green Deal** and **Digital Single Market**, Brexit has demonstrated the difficulties in achieving a truly unified Europe, especially when it comes to the protection of national interests and political autonomy.

For the EU, Brexit has prompted reflection on the future of European integration. While some fear that other countries may follow the UK's example, others see Brexit as an opportunity for the EU to become more coherent and unified in its policies. The EU's response to Brexit, including its negotiations with the UK on issues like trade and security, will likely shape the future of integration and the EU's role on the world stage (BBC News, Foreign Affairs).

3.6. COVID-19 and the Recovery Plan for Europe: Milestone in Fiscal Solidarity

The **COVID-19 pandemic** marked an unprecedented global crisis, not only due to its public health impact but also because of its profound economic and social consequences. For the European Union (EU), the pandemic represented a crucial test of its solidarity mechanisms, as the virus affected all member states, irrespective of their economic strength or social systems. The EU's response to the pandemic, particularly its economic and fiscal measures, highlighted the challenges and potential of **deeper integration**, revealing both the limits of existing frameworks and the possibilities for new forms of cooperation during extraordinary times.

3.6.1. The Economic Impact of COVID-19

The **COVID-19 crisis** led to an economic downturn of historic proportions across the globe. In the EU, strict lockdown measures, border closures, and a halt in economic activity led to sharp contractions in GDP, widespread job losses, and significant disruptions in trade and supply chains. According to the European Commission, EU GDP fell by about 6.3% in 2020, marking the deepest recession in the Union's history. The public health crisis also put immense strain on healthcare systems, while simultaneously exacerbating social inequalities, with the most vulnerable groups suffering the hardest. This crisis highlighted the EU's inability to act with the same speed and efficiency as a single state, particularly in responding to the immediate economic needs of member states.

Each member state adopted its own measures to tackle the crisis, ranging from public health interventions to economic support packages for businesses and individuals. However, these national efforts, while necessary, revealed the limits of the EU's existing economic governance model, which is primarily based on national sovereignty and limited fiscal coordination (European Parliament Research Service, 2020).

3.6.2. NextGenerationEU: A Historic Fiscal Response

In response to the pandemic, the EU introduced **NextGenerationEU**, an unprecedented **recovery package** aimed at addressing the economic fallout and providing the necessary fiscal support for recovery. With an overall value of €750 billion, NextGenerationEU is the largest recovery package ever financed by the EU, representing a bold step toward fiscal solidarity. The plan was designed to provide targeted financial assistance to the hardest-hit countries, focusing on investments in green energy, digitalization, and social resilience (European Commission, 2020).

The recovery fund consisted of two main components:

1. **The Recovery and Resilience Facility (RRF)**, which allocated €672.5 billion in loans and grants to member states to support their national recovery plans. These funds were primarily directed at fostering economic recovery, accelerating the green and digital transitions, and reinforcing social systems to build resilience against future crises (European Parliament Research Service, 2020).
2. **The other components of the package** focused on strengthening the EU's long-term budget, reinforcing the European Investment Bank (EIB), and supporting the European Commission's initiatives in research and development, public health, and crisis response (Bickerton et al., 2020).

3.6.3. Funding Through Common Debt: A Breakthrough in Fiscal Integration

One of the most significant and innovative aspects of NextGenerationEU was that it was funded through **common debt issuance**, an approach that marked a historical departure from the EU's traditional stance on fiscal matters. Traditionally, EU member states were expected to finance their national budgets individually, and any shared funding initiatives were heavily constrained by the **Stability and Growth Pact**, which limited budget deficits and public debt.

NextGenerationEU, however, relied on the European Commission issuing bonds on behalf of the entire EU, effectively borrowing collectively on the international markets. This common issuance of debt, backed by the EU's budget, represented a **milestone in fiscal solidarity**. It marked the first time that the EU as a whole issued debt to finance a recovery plan, thus circumventing the traditional resistance to joint borrowing that had existed for decades. Member states agreed to repay the debt collectively, with no individual country taking responsibility for the debt incurred.

The decision to issue common debt was not without controversy. Countries like **Germany**, the **Netherlands**, and **Austria** were initially hesitant, fearing that joint borrowing could set a dangerous precedent for deeper fiscal integration that would require permanent financial transfers between countries. In contrast, countries such as **Italy** and **Spain**, which were among the hardest hit by the pandemic, argued that the EU should demonstrate solidarity through significant financial support. Ultimately, the German Chancellor **Angela Merkel** played a key role in brokering an agreement on the common debt issuance, reflecting the pragmatic nature of EU decision-making during crises (Bickerton et al., 2020).

3.6.4. Federalist Echoes and the Path Toward Deeper Integration

The fiscal measures taken in response to the COVID-19 crisis have been described as echoing **federalist principles** within the EU. For the first time in EU history, the Union demonstrated a level of **fiscal integration** that had previously been unthinkable, temporarily circumventing the limitations imposed by national sovereignty in favour of collective action. As **NextGenerationEU** was based on common borrowing, it highlighted the EU's ability to act as a collective entity with shared financial responsibility, rather than relying on national governments to independently address crises.

This move was particularly striking because it marked a departure from the EU's usual conservative approach to fiscal policy, which has historically emphasised maintaining national control over budgetary matters. The success of NextGenerationEU, particularly in the context of the pandemic, raised questions about whether this type of **fiscal solidarity** could become a permanent feature of the EU's governance model, potentially paving the way for further integration in areas like tax policy, social welfare, and economic coordination (Armingeon et al., 2022).

For many, the issuance of common debt was a key **turning point** in the EU's trajectory, highlighting the Union's **capacity for deeper integration** in times of crisis. The success of this approach could serve as a model for future crises, where rapid collective action is required to address shared challenges, such as climate change, economic inequality, or technological disruption (Schmitter, 2005).

To conclude, the **COVID-19 pandemic** and the **NextGenerationEU recovery plan** represent a **new era of fiscal solidarity** in the European Union. The EU's decision to issue common debt and provide substantial financial assistance to member states underlines the potential for deeper integration in times of crisis. While challenges remain, particularly in the area of fiscal governance and the distribution of responsibility for debt repayment, NextGenerationEU has demonstrated the EU's capacity for collective action, paving the way for future initiatives aimed at reinforcing the Union's resilience and promoting long-term prosperity.

The success of NextGenerationEU also raises important questions about the future of fiscal policy in the EU. Could this approach to common borrowing become a permanent feature of European economic governance? And if so, how might it impact the balance between national sovereignty and supranational governance in the EU? These questions will likely continue to shape debates about the future direction of European integration in the years to come.

The COVID-19 pandemic represented another turning point. The EU responded with an unprecedented recovery package: NextGenerationEU, amounting to €750 billion. Funded through common debt issuance, the plan marked a milestone in fiscal solidarity.

This move, echoing federalist principles, temporarily circumvented traditional resistance to joint borrowing. Although exceptional, it revealed the potential for deeper fiscal integration in times of crisis.

Thus, while the European Union has made substantial evolutions in its institutional development and policy integration since 2006, it faces ongoing challenges that threaten its unity. Internal fragmentation, political polarisation, and external geopolitical divisions all pose significant risks to the EU's cohesion. As the Union face these challenges, its future will depend on its ability to balance deepening integration in certain areas with addressing the growing divisions within its member states. The EU's capacity to remain united in the face of these challenges will determine its future as a global actor.

Since 2006, the EU has experienced both centripetal and centrifugal forces. While crises have exposed fault lines, they have also driven innovation in governance and reinforced the necessity of cooperation. The hybrid nature of the EU, partly intergovernmental, partly supranational, has become more pronounced, suggesting that future integration will likely follow a flexible, multi-speed path balancing unity and diversity.

4. Romania and the European Union: A Case Study in Post-Accession Integration

Romania's accession to the European Union on January 1, 2007, marked a significant milestone in both the country's post-communist transformation and the EU's eastern enlargement (Vachudova, 2005; Grabbe, 2006). This chapter explores Romania's path within the Union after 2006, focusing on how the country has engaged with and contributed to the evolving process of European integration (Tănăsescu, 2009). It also aims to examine how integration theories—particularly those related to Europeanization, conditionality, and post-accession compliance—apply to Romania's experience, highlighting both alignment and divergence from theoretical models (Schimmelfennig & Sedelmeier, 2005; Papadimitriou & Gateva, 2009).

4.1. The Accession Context and Immediate Post-Accession Period

The EU's 2007 enlargement was widely regarded as a geopolitical imperative and a strategic measure to promote stability, security, and economic development in Eastern Europe (Vachudova, 2005). Romania's accession, while symbolically significant, also underscored persistent concerns regarding the country's administrative capacity and rule of law. As a result, Romania—along with Bulgaria—entered the Union under the conditional framework of the Cooperation and Verification Mechanism (CVM), an unprecedented post-accession monitoring tool designed to ensure progress in judicial reform and anti-corruption measures (Papadimitriou & Gateva, 2009). This differentiated approach reflected a broader shift in EU integration policy, from pre-accession conditionality to ongoing supervision, highlighting the Union's evolving strategies for maintaining coherence and credibility among member states (Grabbe, 2006; Schimmelfennig & Sedelmeier, 2005).

Despite the constraints imposed by the CVM, Romania has used its EU membership as leverage to pursue reforms and enhance its international profile. However, the uneven pace of domestic transformation and the persistence of structural weaknesses have continued to challenge the country's full alignment with EU standards. These dynamics raise important questions about the effectiveness of conditionality beyond accession and the applicability of integration theories—particularly Europeanization and rational choice institutionalism—in post-accession contexts (Tănăsescu, 2009).

Romania's accession to the European Union on January 1, 2007, marked the culmination of a complex transition from a centrally planned economy to a functioning market democracy. As a case study in post-accession integration, Romania provides valuable insights into the opportunities, challenges, and policy dynamics faced by newer member states. The impact of the EU integration on Romania across political, economic, and social dimensions emphasises the interconnection between national strategies and EU-level processes.

4.1.1. Institutional and Legal Alignment

Following accession, Romania undertook substantial reforms to align its legal and institutional frameworks with the acquis communautaire. This process was monitored through the Cooperation and Verification Mechanism (CVM), which specifically targeted improvements in judicial reform, anti-corruption efforts, and the rule of law (European Commission, 2007). Introduced as a post-accession safeguard, the CVM reflected the EU's concerns that Romania's legal and institutional frameworks required continued oversight even after formal accession. Despite early signs of progress, persistent concerns remained regarding the independence of the judiciary and the influence of political actors on legal institutions (Papadimitriou & Gateva, 2009). Periodic CVM reports documented a mixed trajectory—highlighting institutional achievements, while also pointing to recurring challenges such as selective justice, politicized anti-corruption campaigns, and slow implementation of structural reforms (European Commission, 2018). These developments underscored the complexities of sustaining reform momentum within a fluctuating and sometimes resistant domestic political context, raising broader questions about the limits of EU leverage once membership has been granted (Grabbe, 2006; Tănăsescu, 2009).

4.1.2. Economic Convergence and Structural Funds

EU membership brought substantial financial support to Romania, making it one of the largest beneficiaries of structural and cohesion funds within the Union. These investments have been directed toward critical sectors such as infrastructure, rural development, education, and innovation (European Commission, 2020). Financial assistance under the EU's multiannual financial frameworks contributed to reducing development gaps and enhancing Romania's integration into the single market. However, while macroeconomic indicators reflect notable progress, Romania's GDP per capita rose from around 40% of the EU average in 2007 to over 70% by 2023, significant regional disparities remain, particularly between urban and rural areas and between regions like Bucharest-Ilfov and the North-East (Eurostat, 2023). Moreover, although absorption rates for EU funds improved in successive budget cycles, they were often constrained by bureaucratic inefficiencies, limited administrative capacity at the local level, and complex regulatory frameworks (Dobre, 2021; Bachtler & Mendez, 2016). These factors continue to influence the effectiveness of EU investment in fostering balanced and inclusive economic convergence.

4.1.3. Migration, Labour Mobility, and Demographic Challenges

Since Romania acceded to the European Union in 2007, migration has become one of the most significant socio-economic phenomena shaping the country's development trajectory. The promise of higher wages, better employment opportunities, and improved living standards in Western Europe led to large-scale emigration, particularly among young and educated individuals. By 2022, estimates indicated that over 3.5 million Romanians, roughly 17% of the country's population, were living abroad, making Romania one of the largest countries of origin for intra-EU migration (OECD, 2022; World Bank, 2018). The primary destinations included Italy, Spain, Germany, and the United Kingdom, facilitated by the EU's principle of free movement.

While remittances from the diaspora have played a stabilising role, contributing approximately 2–3% of GDP annually, they cannot fully offset the long-term structural effects of mass emigration. The country has experienced labour shortages in key sectors such as healthcare, construction, and agriculture, as well as declining school enrollment rates and rural depopulation (Roman & Vasilescu, 2016). Moreover, the loss of highly skilled professionals, particularly doctors and IT specialists, has intensified concerns about a persistent brain drain and the state's capacity to deliver public services.

More recently, Romania has also seen patterns of **return migration**, especially during the COVID-19 pandemic and amid shifting labour dynamics across Europe. However, reintegration remains a challenge due to underdeveloped institutional support and mismatches between returnees' skills and local labour market needs (Anghel et al., 2016). Romania's experience highlights the need for coherent national policies on diaspora engagement, labour market adaptation, and demographic resilience, as well as for targeted EU support aimed at addressing mobility-related asymmetries within the Union.

Romania's accession to the European Union significantly accelerated labour migration, as the lifting of mobility restrictions enabled millions of Romanian citizens to seek employment in countries such as Italy, Spain, Germany, and the United Kingdom (Geddes & Scholten, 2016). While this outward migration contributed positively through remittances, which became an important source of household income and supported domestic consumption, the phenomenon also triggered negative consequences, including a substantial brain drain and long-term demographic decline, particularly in rural and economically disadvantaged regions (Anghel et al., 2016).

This duality illustrates a core tension within the European integration project: while enhanced labour mobility promotes individual economic opportunity and transnational connectivity, it can also exacerbate structural vulnerabilities in sending countries by depleting human capital and weakening local labour markets (Barslund & Busse, 2016). Romania's case highlights the need for complementary national and EU-level strategies to mitigate the adverse effects of mobility, including reintegration policies, investments in human capital, and regional development programs targeting left-behind communities.

4.2. Romania's Role in Shaping EU Policy

While Romania's initial participation in the European Union was largely reactive, focused primarily on aligning with acquis communautaire and fulfilling post-accession requirements, recent years have marked a shift toward more proactive and strategic engagement in EU policymaking (Tănăsescu, 2009; Gheciu, 2018). A turning point in this trajectory was Romania's 2019 Presidency of the Council of the European Union, during which it emphasised key priorities such as cohesion, convergence, connectivity, and common values. The Presidency showcased Romania's administrative capacity and diplomatic maturity, as it managed over 2,500 events and negotiated numerous legislative files amid a challenging institutional climate shaped by Brexit and the approaching European elections (European Council, 2019).

Beyond its institutional role, Romanian policymakers have increasingly engaged in shaping EU debates on critical issues, including migration, enlargement, and energy security. The war in Ukraine further underscored Romania's strategic importance. Positioned at the EU's eastern border and sharing close linguistic, historical, and political ties with Moldova and Ukraine, Romania has emerged as a vocal supporter of Ukraine's European path and has facilitated humanitarian and logistical assistance through border and port infrastructure (Brinza, 2022). Romania has also taken an active stance in promoting the EU enlargement agenda for the Western Balkans and Moldova, reinforcing its role as a bridge between the EU and its eastern neighbourhood.

In parallel, Romania has intensified advocacy for its own deeper integration within the Schengen Area. Although it met technical criteria for accession as early as 2011, political hurdles, mainly related to rule-of-law concerns and broader EU dynamics, have delayed membership. Nonetheless, Romania's consistent diplomatic efforts, support for EU unity in times of crisis, and alignment with common foreign and security policy demonstrate a maturing strategic posture within the Union (Bărbulescu & Troncotă, 2020). As Romania continues to develop its administrative, diplomatic, and normative capacities, its contribution to shaping EU policy, particularly in Eastern Europe, is likely to expand further.

Romania's post-accession journey reflects both the promises and the complexities of EU integration. While significant strides have been made in legal alignment, economic modernisation, and regional cooperation, persistent governance challenges and socio-economic disparities remain. Romania's case underscores the importance of sustained institutional commitment, strategic vision, and inclusive policymaking to fully harness the transformative potential of European integration.

Bibliography

1. Armingeon, K., de la Porte, C., Heins, E. et al. Voices from the past: economic and political vulnerabilities in the making of next generation EU. Comp Eur Polit 20, 144–165 (2022). https://doi.org/10.1057/s41295-022-00277-6.
2. Bachtler, J., & Mendez, C. (2016). EU Cohesion Policy and European Integration: The Dynamics of EU Budget and Regional Policy Reform. Palgrave Macmillan.
3. Bărbulescu, I. G., & Troncotă, M. (2020). Romania and the Schengen saga: Between technical compliance and political conditionality. European Politics and Society, 21(1), 134–149. https://doi.org/10.1080/23745118.2019.1571751.
4. Berstein, Serge; Milza Pierre. Istoria Europei - Secolul XX (din 1919 până în zilele noastre), volumul 5. Iaşi. Institutul European pentru Cooperare Cultural-Ştiinţifică, 1998.
5. Beerkens, M. and Vossensteyn, H. (2011). The effect of the Erasmus programme on European higher education, 45-62. https://doi.org/10.1007/978-94-6091-555-0_4.
6. Bickerton, C., Hodson, D., & Puetter, U. (2014). The New Intergovernmentalism: European Integration in the post-Maastricht era. JCMS Journal of Common Market Studies, 53(4), 703-722. https://doi.org/10.1111/jcms.12212.
7. Brack, N., Coman, R., & Crespy, A. (2019). Unpacking old and new conflicts of sovereignty in the European polity. Journal of European Integration, 41(7), 817-832. https://doi.org/10.1080/07036337.2019.1665657.
8. Brinza, A. (2022). Romania's role in supporting Ukraine: From border state to strategic gateway. European Council on Foreign Relations. https://ecfr.eu.
9. Chugunov, D., Kasyanov, R., & Evdokimov, M. (2023). Comprehension of the EU political and legal development. Kutafin Law Review, 9(4), 713-739. https://doi.org/10.17803/2313-5395.2022.4.22.713-739.
10. Dinan, D. (2016). Governance and institutions: a more political commission. JCMS Journal of Common Market Studies, 54(S1), 101-116. https://doi.org/10.1111/jcms.12427.
11. Dobre, A. (2021). Administrative capacity and the absorption of EU funds in Romania: Challenges and prospects. Romanian Journal of European Affairs, 21(1), 34–49.

12.Dodescu, Anca. Economia integrării Europene. Oradea. Editura Universităţii din Oradea, 2004.
13.Ellinas, A. and Suleiman, E. (2011). Supranationalism in a transnational bureaucracy: the case of the European Commission. JCMS Journal of Common Market Studies, 49(5), 923-947. https://doi.org/10.1111/j.1468-5965.2010.02164.x
14.Etzioni, A. (1965). Political Unification: A Comparative Study of Leaders and Forces. Holt, Rinehart and Winston.
15.Hoffmann, Stanley. Sisiful European. Studii despre Europa (1964 – 1994). Bucureşti. Editura Curtea Veche, 2003.
16.Georgiou, C. (2021). Europe's 'Hamiltonian moment'? on the political uses and explanatory usefulness of a recurrent historical comparison. Economy and Society, 51(1), 138-159. https://doi.org/10.1080/03085147.2021.1968676.
17.Genschel, P. and Jachtenfuchs, M. (2015). More integration, less federation: the European integration of core state powers. Journal of European Public Policy, 23(1), 42-59. https://doi.org/10.1080/13501763.2015.1055782.
18.Gheciu, A. (2018). Security governance in East-Central Europe: The emergence of a new European security order? In A. Gheciu & W. Wohlforth (Eds.), The Oxford Handbook of International Security (pp. 516–532). Oxford University Press.
19.Goldsmith, M. (2003). Variable geometry, multilevel governance: European integration and subnational government in the new millennium., 112-133. https://doi.org/10.1093/0199252092.003.0005.
20.Grabbe, H. (2006). The EU's transformative power: Europeanization through conditionality in Central and Eastern Europe. Palgrave Macmillan.
21.Haas, E. B. (1958). *The Uniting of Europe: Political, Social, and Economic Forces* (2nd ed.). Stanford University Press.
22.Haas, E. B. (1964). *Beyond the Nation-State: Functionalism and International Organization*. Stanford University Press.
23.Haas, E. B. (1970). *The Study of Regional Integration: A Theoretical Overview. International Organization*, 24(4), 607-646.
24.Hamilton, A. (1787). *Federalist No. 9: The Union as a Safeguard Against Domestic Faction and Insurrection*. In *The Federalist Papers*. Retrieved from https://www.congress.gov/resources/display/content/The+Federalist+Papers#TheFederalistPapers-9.
25.Harbers, I., Tatham, M., Tillin, L., & Zuber, C. (2021). Thirty years of regional and federal studies. Regional & Federal Studies, 31(1), 1-23. https://doi.org/10.1080/13597566.2020.1868998.

26.Kohler-Koch, B. and Friedrich, D. (2019). Business interest in the EU: integration without supranationalism?. JCMS Journal of Common Market Studies, 58(2), 455-471. https://doi.org/10.1111/jcms.12929.

27.Majone, G. (1994). *The Rise of the Regulatory State in Europe. West European Politics*, 17(3), 77–101.

28.Marga, A. (2003). Filosofia unificării europene. Cluj-Napoca. Editura Fundaţiei pentru Studii Europene.

29.Mitrany, D. (1943). A Working Peace System: An Argument for the Functional Development of International Organization. London: Royal Institute of International Affairs.

30.Monnet, J. (1978). Memoirs (R. Mayne, Trans.). Doubleday. (Original work published 1976)

31.Morin, E. (2002). Gândind Europa. Bucureşti. Editura Trei.

32.Митин, A. and Lebedev, D. (2024). Risks of loss of state sovereignty and balance of interests under the influence of aggressive forms of supranational control. European and Asian Law Review, 10-23. https://doi.org/10.34076/27821668_2024_7_1_10.

33.Papadimitriou, D., & Gateva, E. (2009). Assessing the performance of EU conditionality in South East Europe: The case of Bulgaria and Romania. European Political Science Review, 1(3), 379–401. https://doi.org/10.1017/S1755773909990152.

34.Păun, N., Păun, A. C., Ciceo, G. (2003). Europa unită, Europa noastră. Cluj-Napoca.Editura Presa Universitară Clujeană.

35.Pecican, O. (1999). Europa o idee în mers. Cluj-Napoca. Editura Limes.

36.Perrings, C., Hechter, M., & Mamada, R. (2021). National polarisation and international agreements. Proceedings of the National Academy of Sciences, 118(50). https://doi.org/10.1073/pnas.2102145118.

37.Popovici, A. (2010). David Mitrany and Functionalism: The Beginnings of Functionalism. Review of Research and Social Intervention, 1, 163–179.

38.Powers, K. (2022). Conclusions, 205-236. https://doi.org/10.23943/princeton/9780691224572.003.0006.

39.Rittberger, B. (2003). The creation and empowerment of the European Parliament*. JCMS Journal of Common Market Studies, 41(2), 203-225. https://doi.org/10.1111/1468-5965.00419

40.Risse, T. (2014). No demos? Identities and Public Spheres in the Euro Crisis. JCMS Journal of Common Market Studies, 52(6), 1207-1215. https://doi.org/10.1111/jcms.12189.

41. Schmeer, L. (2023). The establishment of the European Public Prosecutor's office: integration with limited supranationalisation?. Journal of European Integration, 45(6), 845-869. https://doi.org/10.1080/07036337.2023.2196069.
42. Schraff, D. (2020). Is the member states' curse the EU's blessing? inequality and eu regime evaluation. JCMS Journal of Common Market Studies, 58(5), 1215-1234. https://doi.org/10.1111/jcms.13027.
43. Schmitter, P. C. (2005). The Mechanisms of European Integration. European Political Science Review, 1(1), 13-32.
44. Schimmelfennig, F., & Sedelmeier, U. (Eds.). (2005). The Europeanization of Central and Eastern Europe. Cornell University Press.
45. Smith, K. E. (2004). Politica externă a Uniunii Europene. Bucureşti. Editura Trei.
46. Souliotis, N., Alexandri, G. (2016). From Embedded to Uncompromising Neoliberalism: Competitiveness Policies and European Union Interscalar Relations in the Case of Greece. European Urban and Regional Studies, 24(3), 227-240. https://doi.org/10.1177/0969776416630582.
47. Tănăsescu, E. S. (2009). Romania's EU accession: Between formal adoption and substantive implementation of the acquis. Romanian Journal of European Affairs, 9(2), 5–24.
48. Toshkov, D. (2011). Public Opinion and Policy Output in the European Union: A Lost Relationship. European Union Politics, 12(2), 169-191. https://doi.org/10.1177/1465116510395043.
49. Vachudova, M. A. (2005). Europe undivided: Democracy, leverage, and integration after communism. Oxford University Press.
50. Verovšek, P. (2014). Unexpected support for European integration: memory, rupture, and totalitarianism in Arendt's political theory. The Review of Politics, 76(3), 389-413. https://doi.org/10.1017/s0034670514000308.
51. Zorgbibe, Charles. Construcţia europeană. Trecut, prezent, viitor. Bucureşti. Editura Trei, 1998.
52. Wyn Jones, R. & T. Houghton. (2019). The Politics of Brexit: The Challenge of European Integration. Cambridge University Press.

Sites

European Commission. (2020). *The European Green Deal*. European Commission. Retrieved from https://ec.europa.eu/info/strategy/priorities-2019-2024/european-green-deal_en

European Commission. (2020). *The European Semester: Economic Governance for Growth and Stability*. European Commission. Retrieved from https://ec.europa.eu/info/business-economy-euro/economic-and-fiscal-policy-coordination/european-semester_en

European Union. (2020). *EU Enlargement: The History of Enlargement*. European Union. Retrieved from https://europa.eu/european-union/about-eu/history_en

European Commission. (2020). *New Pact on Migration and Asylum*. Retrieved from https://ec.europa.eu/info/strategy/priorities-2019-2024/promoting-our-european-way-life/new-pact-migration-and-asylum_en

Frontex (2020). *Frontex: European Border and Coast Guard Agency*. Retrieved from https://frontex.europa.eu/

European Parliament Research Service. (2020). *EU Migration Policy: A Turning Point?*. Retrieved from https://www.europarl.europa.eu/thinktank/en/home.html

Migration Watch UK. (2015). *The Migration Crisis: Policy Response and Impact*. Retrieved from https://www.migrationwatchuk.org/

BBC News. (2020). *Brexit: Timeline of Key Events*. Retrieved from https://www.bbc.com/news/uk-politics-32810887

The Migration Observatory. (2020). *UK Migration Statistics and Trends*. Oxford University. Retrieved from https://migrationobservatory.ox.ac.uk

European Council on Foreign Relations. (2020). *The EU and the Migration Crisis: A Fragmented Response*. Retrieved from https://ecfr.eu

European Commission. (2020). *European Structural and Investment Funds – Country Report: Romania*. https://ec.europa.eu

Eurostat. (2023). *Regional GDP per capita compared to the EU average*. https://ec.europa.eu/eurostat

European Council. (2019). *Romanian Presidency of the Council of the EU – Main achievements*. https://www.consilium.europa.eu

Webpages

1. http://www.mfe.it/gfe
2. http://www.romacivica.net
3. http://www.europeana.ro
4. http://idd.euro.ubbcluj.ro
5. http://www.geocities.com
6. http://www.mie.ro
7. http://www.mae.ro
8. http://www.ier.ro
9. http://www.infoeuropa.ro
10. http://www.gardianul.ro
11. http://www.esc.eu.int/
12. http://www.eurativ.com/
13. http://www.eurunion.org
14. http://www.ue.eu.int.
15. http://www.insight.eun.org
16. http://www.europrix.org
17. http://www.citizens.eu.int
18. http://www.euobserver.com
19. http://www.europa.eu.int
20. http://www.europarl.eu.int
21. http://www.cor.eu
22. http://www.dadalos-europe.org
23. http://www.e-europeanawards.org
24. http://www.Europen.com
25. http://www.ifj-europe.org
26. http://www.publicinfo.ro
27. http://www.transparency.org.ro
28. http://www.ecb.int/
29. http://www.clube.ro
30. http://www.eib.org/

www.ingramcontent.com/pod-product-compliance
Lightning Source LLC
LaVergne TN
LVHW022317200926
848481LV00004B/1369